Bar Fights with Sad Kids

poems by

Melina Cohen-Bramwell

Finishing Line Press
Georgetown, Kentucky

Bar Fights with Sad Kids

Publisher: Leah Huete de Maines
Editor: Christen Kincaid
Cover Art: Photo by Dan Counsell
Author Photo: Melina Cohen-Bramwell
Cover Design: Elizabeth Maines McCleavy

Order online: www.finishinglinepress.com
also available on amazon.com

Author inquiries and mail orders:
Finishing Line Press
PO Box 1626
Georgetown, Kentucky 40324
USA

Contents

Part One:
The View from Outside the Bar

San Francisco

This city smells like cigarettes
booze and despair
perfume in her hair as she walks by
smiles at me
so I know she's not crying
so I know she's not lying *have a nice day*
Welcome to the city
Thirteen's eighteen here
Beauty's fleeting here
The air's intoxicated waiting for a moment to break
the tension and fear
I can hear it in your voice
You're not telling the truth
You just want some juice
some city Nyquil you might as well it's something to do
I can't stop you by walking by
I can't stop you cause time flies on and on
and we've all fallen on some hard times
We're all pregnant and starving in our own minds
Soaking up the stench of piss and cigarette smoke
as we pass by and gloat
our lives suck too but at least we're not you

A Birthday Surprise
(from your fifteen-year-old)

I could get you a card
only paper that says
this is more important than the words I say everyday
I love you
but this makes it true

I could get you a gift
You can hold it cold
no emotion any devotion in my heart is
shallow as this tactile stab in the back
this thing for one brief moment you feel you lack
is how important you are to me

I could get you a bouquet
clump of pretty flowers you watch shrivel away
to remind you life is short
Life is ephemeral
It will be over before you know it
Happy birthday

Mulatto

When he started listening to trap music he started getting tougher
street-smart gangsta rougher
He looked around and realized he was black
but he knew he couldn't rap
so he grabbed another can of liquid hope from the kitchen cabinet

He saw he didn't fit in so he cast off his skin
In his dreams he was lighter and lighter
acting whiter and whiter
acculturation assimilation integration
But the story the mirror told was flying off the shelves
and when he opened his mouth people still stared

cherries

cherries fallen from a tree
squished under careless feet
their scent like a worm infecting the air
infecting the blood
in the street
a quiet morning
woman running down with bags in hand
dragging three-year-old behind
you see them coming
waving at you to
hold up be patient care
but you pull out
and leave them at the bus stop
waiting
an hour not too long
but for the kid
tired sick and hungry
clinging to his mother's arm
to him you're just another rotten cherry

We Don't Party Too Hard
(to a child-actor I once knew)

I should worry about myself
and my new options:
shit forever death or sobriety
Instead I'm worried about society
raising you like a mother

You and the other little girls
circled me on break asking
do you party?
With role-models like me
it won't be long
before you're filling chairs at this
30 under 30 AA meeting

Youth's not innocence
At least neither of us were
It's just jazz hands and smiles while the lights are hot

As I exit I can see you
entering this tunnel
following tracks that break off
in only three directions
shining pewter in your eager eyes
all bedazzled with their caution signs

a symphony of the animate

a symphony of the animate
a sonata of restless sleep

hands clinging to the thoughts we dare not speak

I'm giddy and silly with our languid calm
connected palm to palm
for once in this lonely world

we quiet our sounds
not to disturb the peace

the serenity caresses my cheek

and for this moment fleeting and complete
I am content

California Doesn't Have Rivers

I don't know why you hate me but I despise you for it

with your tiny arms and spite-smushed face

your skillful humor and sticky charm

One day I'll be popular

and everyone will like me

and then you'll have to like me

cause you're insecure too

Brother

(to the memory loss induced by your suicide attempt)

Maybe you don't remember now
how you're a part of me
and I'm a part of you

How out of slinkies and prop-rings
paper and black strings
we made a bridge that can't be burnt
I can't hold up without you

These past two years gone
by and lost in your new void
dark as the closet tight as your rope

Now I need oxygen I need hope

that you remember what you said to me then
when from the gurney I strapped in called you
coughing sticky ash and Tylenol

I love you
Those thoughts are not true

I want happiness to find you too

and I'll wait
till time has passed we've done it all again
cause I remember
and I'll remember
and I'll wait

Clean

Washing you out of my bedsheets

Brushing you out of my teeth

My fingertips leave indentations on your body

My tongue is sucking you to sleep

My fingertips leave dirty streaks across your body

prints I can't get off you in the wash

Your fingertips make filthy trails across my body

Covered in your grease that soap can't thin

I'm stripping you off of my skin

On the train I feel you clawing up the back of my throat

On the bus I smell you lingering on my chin

The doctors test if you are in my bloodstream

if pills will clean this mess up I slipped in

The doctors test if you are in my bloodstream

while I burn the memory of you off my lips

The doctors test if you are in my bloodstream

while I imagine someone else was my first kiss

Part Two:
The View from Inside the Bar

College Kid

He's a three-time PTSD award winner
That's the Pulitzer Prize to the soymilk for dinner
cause we ran out of money for some real shit crowd
We're not faking but they're still
rich-spending-Daddy's-money crowd
grew up with a Daddy crowd
don't realize it's not funny stuck as the caddy
listening to your bullshit about someone else's life crowd
shit about my life
Like you know what's right cause you read it off tumblr
Now you're here rolling Js tossing back tumblers
thinking about nothing
Worried that you're too cool to skip school you break rules
but only the ones that are so last season
Believe in anything convenient
Know when the shit blows over and the dust settles
you're gonna be fine

Birthday SRS

On my twenty-first birthday
I'm on the couch wrapped
in gauze itching from antibiotics

chest resealing from the wounds
I'd paid my savings to inflict
And this is better

I keep saying so my parents
will not dwell on how
if they'd *just done it well*

I'd be their little girl
shining feminine swirl-
ing out the bar

and round the lamppost
and back in with all
my many beautiful friends

Instead of on this couch or
chugging to the C-diff
in the corner of the kitchen

from the bottle
in the secret spot hidden
with all its emptied sisters

Giving toilet tastes
of vodka and amoxicillin
cocktails garnished with dustings
of chewed Vicodin round the rim

Happy birthday to me
Happy birthday to me
Happy birthday dear Melina
And so again it begins

Charley's Chair

I know I told you it didn't make me sad

to see you stuck in that chair

because it makes you happier

and it's easier for you

and you finally feel normal

and able

and free

But it does

because once you didn't need it

and now you do

Now I'm forced to remember that

not just you

Charley's Chair Revision

It was nice to see you so happy
able and free
with your *superpowers*
zipping around the park
with me on your lap
on the verge of tears
because life isn't easy
it never has been
and it's not your fault

But we're together
in happiness and in apathy
in adulthood and in pain
in the simple joy of rolling down
the bumpy sidewalk like brothers

playing with your new toy

sunshower sunday

raindrops in the loitering afternoon sun

glisten on leaves like tinsel

wind rustles hands in children's hair

surrounded on my bed by books

with hardly room for legs

a song escapes my lips like a compulsion

there are days

or moments

when beauty is not far from my fingertips

and happiness

seems just beyond the next hilltop

The Sports Section

I used to save the sports sections

of Mommy's *New York Times*

so when you came over I could give them to you

all at once

as one big sports newspaper

I remember the day you told me you cheated on her

that you had broken up

and wanted me to meet your girlfriend

I was crying in the corner

holding your sports newspaper

trying to force on a smile so I could hand it to you

I don't remember if I did

I Fill My Stomach and Then I Drink
(to Daddy and his latest girlfriend)

I fill my stomach and then I drink she said
I just can't help it
I fill my stomach and then I drink
over and over
in her house with the plastic solo cups
and the plastic dishes
and a TV in every room
a TV in the living room
a TV in the kitchen you mounted
which you can hear from the bathroom you fixed
But you don't care about her at all
or maybe anyone
but especially not her

Yet you brought me here to stay in her house
and eat in her kitchen
with the garbage full of plastic cups and plastic dishes
and the TV blaring 24/7
You brought me here cause it makes her feel important
or it makes you seem important
or cause it buys you time
to stay in her house and eat the food she makes
off her disposable plastic dishes
until you find a way to throw her away with them

Fag

A dispatch from this blank-walled room
with my twitching cat
where we wait like refugees from paternal indifference:

We need plates
and a heater might be nice
though I declined the one they offered me

I ate the lunch my mom packed me
while thinking about my ancestors in the Underground Railroad
hiding from the Nazis in attics
how many lonely blank walls they must have stared at
while shivering on stained futons
comforting their trembling cats
And how the atrocity I'm running from is
but one word

Hearing Evil Brew on Live TV

My mother is downstairs listening to Trump speak at the RNC
She says she's interested in the psychological implications
She has a PHD in that
I can hear the crowd chanting
hear them whistle and roar through the TV downstairs
and it feels like I'm in a movie
about the apocalypse
The dissonant minor of their unison cheers
portending the end of the world
I can plug my ears and say la la la
I can't hear you
but like everyone who does that
I actually can

R.I.P. Jay Catsby

I made an appointment with death
for you I marked it in our mutual calendar
1:15 at the VCA across the street

When it rains it pours
and it floods out our storm drains
and city muck flows like rivers
down asphalt streets
fire damaged hills slide towards the ocean
and we all drown
paws curling and hands grasping
lungs gasping for air
It's all water
All the way down

Taco Tuesday

I'm lying on the boardwalk where I grew up

where I used to throw rocks over the railing to watch the ripples
and looked for black charcoal to make obsidian arrowheads

face down on the wooden planks
half hanging off the edge
spitting up the last drips of acid left in my stomach

Time has slowed down and I'm immobilized
Gravity has multiplied a hundredfold

I see death approaching in the blurry face of the moon
I look him in the eye and I am not afraid
for I invited him here

and I slur my disappointment when he turns away

Shower Poem—Morbid Fascination

I'm in love with all the dying art forms

because their glory has faded into yesteryear

the pall of mortality is on their horizon

and it's important to have something in common with your lovers

I was in the shower when I thought of this poem

half my hair finger-combed the other half dampened and puffy

and I rushed out

dripping all over the carpet and the page

to jot it down

A poem no one will read

because either I or poetry will die before they get to it

Shower Poem Part Two— Best Friend

When I had that anxiety attack

and thought

this is the end
this is it an accidental overdose

When you didn't even know

I was on drugs

and drunk

How could I protect you from that

if I was dead

in your roommate's bed

Why Did You Do This to Me
(no honor amongst thieves)

There's no balm for this sore throat screaming
booze poured out
suicide and Vicodin brushed off the table like breadcrumbs
but I'm on my knees and from the dust on the floor
perhaps I could construct a loaf

Musicality is a Trojan Horse
civility a farce for those more skilled at smiling
with friends they can depend upon
who wear straight hair in tight buns
and are counted when they enter the door

I run with stray dogs
and when rations are low
they turn their teeth on my flesh
and with rabid famished jaws they snap my bones

The Lucky Ones

I envy their quiet
no new beginnings their
every sunrise\sunset
same peaceful nothing

I envy children
plucked from life
when they're ripe
before their wax melts
shellacs the candelabra
snuffed out spitting smoke
into darkness released
when labors barely started

I think of drowning
when I think of freedom

When I was twelve
I thought Sylvia Plath
baked herself to death like a cake

Melt-

1. ing

all poems sound the same
all poems sound the same
rattle rattle in my brain
all the words they sound the same
all the words they are the sound
are the roar the screech the pound
all the sounds they are the same
all the poems sound the same

2. Down

All work and no play is work
for dull boys play this game
till the well runs dry and you
run cry *I was never invited*
I was never excited since the
sixth grade fantasies ferment
in rotting brain and absence
makes the heart grow absent
presence makes the mind distracted
smile cause you've always acted
shocked when it won't work out
You can get tired of anything Melina
You were born tired

The Tape Fairy

I had to tape over the holes in my screen
so the mosquitos wouldn't get in

Shirtless sun breathing on my chest
I knelt in my window ripping
little pieces of golden gauze for each puncture wound

I was worried the dressings
would ruin the view
from my pillow
of tree-top and sky

But the golden speckles are magic in the twilight hours
The tape fairy dust mystifies my captivity
a suburban fantasy
Released into the magically real

I'm Starting to See the Beauty in Deterioration

As we grew together
so too shall we shrink
In the air of winter mornings creaking joints will stiffen
our topography textured now by lines and hunches
once reserved for futures distant as fiction
and we'll forget the phrases
we giggled over school lunches

The same maples and redwoods
peer down on it all
and the palms drop their fronds
for the next round of midnight youths
leafed rapiers drawn over a moment in time
brief as a pixel in this portrait
coloring a speckle on its brow

The sun will bleach us all
Only dawn awaits us now

MRI Melody

The clean wet air
laundered by rain
the night in sharp relief
my head that only hurts a little
post-scan and re-stirred
hair dancing in the wind
caressing my face in pirouette
lit by stage-light stoplights

And on the inhale
the city feels like mine again
quiet wet pavement
the muffled hip-hop of passing cars
a bar just far enough away
that when I turn
I can't smell the smoke
or hear the voices
of the leaning twenty-something's

The streetlights bat their eyelashes
LED blue
electric possibility
hair blowing in the wind

Melina Cohen-Bramwell, is a writer and lifelong San Francisco Bay Area resident who also happens to be a mixed-race, gender-queer, spoonie. Never a fan of the education system, at age sixteen, Melina dropped out of school and began a career in theater. After years of working as a technician at regional theater companies such as Aurora, Cal Shakes, and Berkeley Rep, Melina "retired" to focus on healing from chronic illness and pursuing writing as a profession. His play, *Good White Men*, was developed by Theatre First of Berkeley, California, in 2019. His play, *Please Don't Slow Me Down*, was workshopped in PlayGround SF's 2023 Free Play Festival. In 2022, development of his play *One of the Good Ones* was featured at Theater Battery in Washington State and, in 2024, at PlayGround SF's 2024 Free Play Festival. He believes one of art's most satisfying functions is to give and receive vulnerability, and he is excited to share this little collection of vulnerable words with you.